MONUMENTAL MILESTONES
GREAT EVENTS OF MODERN TIMES

The Civil Rights Movement

A movement that changed America.

Mitchell Lane
PUBLISHERS

P.O. Box 196
Hockessin, Delaware 19707

Titles in the Series

The Dawn of Aviation:
The Story of the Wright Brothers

Pearl Harbor and the War with Japan

Breaking the Sound Barrier:
The Story of Chuck Yeager

Top Secret: The Story of the
Manhattan Project

The Story of the Holocaust

The Civil Rights Movement

Exploring the North Pole:
The Story of Robert Edwin
Peary and Matthew Henson

The Story of the Great Depression

The Cuban Missile Crisis:
The Cold War Goes Hot

The Fall of the Berlin Wall

Disaster in the Indian Ocean,
Tsunami 2004

MONUMENTAL MILESTONES
GREAT EVENTS OF MODERN TIMES

The Civil Rights Movement

A movement that changed America.

Rebecca Thatcher Murcia

Printing   1   2   3   4   5   6   7   8

   Library of Congress Cataloging-in-Publication Data

Murcia, Rebecca Thatcher, 1962–
    The civil rights movement / by Rebecca Thatcher Murcia
        p. cm. — (Monumental milestones)
    Includes bibliographical references and index.
    ISBN 1-58415-401-2 (library bound)
    1. King, Martin Luther, Jr., 1929–1968—Juvenile literature. 2. African Americans—Biography—Juvenile literature. 3. Civil rights workers—United States—Biography—Juvenile literature. 4. Baptists—United States—Clergy—Biography—Juvenile literature. 5. African Americans—Civil rights—History—Modern times—Juvenile literature. 6. Civil rights movements—United States—History—Modern times—Juvenile literature. I. Title. II. Series.
E185.97.K5M863 2005
323'.092—dc22   2004024609

ABOUT THE AUTHOR: Rebecca Thatcher Murcia has been interested in the civil rights movement since she was a child and her mother told her about the Montgomery bus boycott as a bedtime story. She grew up in Garrison, New York, and went to the University of Massachusetts at Amherst. There, shortly before his death, writer James Baldwin taught the history of the civil rights movement and emphasized that any discussion of civil rights must begin with slavery and the Middle Passage. Murcia now lives in Akron, Pennsylvania, with her husband and two sons, Mario and Gabriel. This is Murcia's fifth book for Mitchell Lane Publishers.

PHOTO CREDITS: Cover, pp. 1, 3, 6, 16, 17, 30, 38, 40—Library of Congress; pp. 8, 10—Corbis; p. 12—Son of the South; p. 18—History Images; pp. 20, 26—Americas Library/Library of Congress; p. 28—Civil Rights Movement Veterans Org.; p. 36—Middle Passage Museum.

PUBLISHER'S NOTE: This story is based on the author's extensive research, which she believes to be accurate. Documentation of such research is contained on page 47.

The internet sites referenced herein were active as of the publication date. Due to the fleeting nature of some web sites, we cannot guarantee they will all be active when you are reading this book.

Contents

The Civil Rights Movement

Rebecca Thatcher Murcia

Chapter 1   Bloody Sunday in Selma 7

FYInfo*: *To Kill a Mockingbird* 11

Chapter 2   Why Civil Rights? 13

FYInfo: *Brown v. Board of Education* 19

Chapter 3   The Birth of a Non-Violent Revolution ... 21

FYInfo: James Baldwin 29

Chapter 4   Violence and Voting 31

FYInfo: Bernice Johnson Reagon 37

Chapter 5   The Rise of Extremes 39

FYInfo: Malcolm X 42

Chronology 43

Timeline in History 44

Chapter Notes 45

Glossary 46

For Further Reading 47

For Young Adults 47

Works Consulted 47

On the Internet 47

Index 48

*For Your Information

"Registering to vote is an act of commitment to the American ideal," John Lewis, one of the leaders of the Civil Rights Movement, said in his 1964 speech. "It is patriotic."

Lewis and other protestors demanding the right to vote were brutally attacked by police on what became known as "Bloody Sunday" in Selma, Alabama, on March 7, 1965. The way the marchers were treated shocked the president and led to the passing of a landmark voting rights law.

Bloody Sunday in Selma

John Lewis stood at one end of the Edmund Pettus Bridge in Selma, Alabama. Behind him was a line of about 600 marchers, dressed as they would for church. But even though it was Sunday morning, March 7, 1965, the marchers weren't going to church.

What we now call the Civil Rights Movement, the quest for equal rights for black Americans, had been going on for more than a decade. There had been victories and losses, successes and failures, but there was still no law guaranteeing the right to vote. Lewis and the others were quietly determined to march to give themselves that right.

They knew it wouldn't be easy. Before them was a sea of helmeted police officers. Some were mounted on horses, while others brandished clubs as big as baseball bats.

There was a moment of indecision. Should the march continue toward the police officers? Another leader of the march, Hosea Williams, asked Lewis if he could swim. It was a long drop down to the river.

"No," Lewis answered.

"Well," Williams said, "neither can I."

"But we might have to,"[1] Lewis responded.

The two men did not stop. They did not succumb to the urge to dive into the river. They continued onto the bridge. Because they believed in non-violence, they kneeled down and began to pray.

The attack was immediate and brutal. The mounted officers had their horses stomp on the marchers. Others attacked and clubbed

John Lewis, left, and Hosea Williams, right, were two organizers of the Civil Rights Movement.

Today, U.S. citizens of all colors take voting rights for granted. Many people do not even bother to go to the polls. During the Civil Rights Movement, activists endured abuse, threats, beatings, and even murder as they fought for the right to vote.

them mercilessly. The officers sprayed a particularly strong kind of tear gas that caused vomiting.

A large state trooper hit Lewis so hard on the side of his head that he felt no pain. He fell to the ground and curled up, trying to protect himself from further blows. He was hit again and the world started to spin.

"I began choking, coughing," Lewis wrote in his memoir. "I couldn't get air into my lungs. I felt as though I was taking my last breath. If there was ever a time in my life for me to panic, it should have been then. But I didn't. I remember how strangely calm I felt as I thought, This is it. People are going to die here. *I'm* going to die here."[2]

The moment of tranquility passed. Lewis began to feel the pain in his head and realized that he could save himself. He got up and looked around. He saw a teen-age boy sitting on the ground with blood gushing from his head. Others were vomiting.

Lewis began the retreat back across the bridge as the attacks continued. He heard people screaming. One woman shouted, "Please, *no!*" Another cried, "We're being *killed!*"[3]

Still the attacks continued. The officers followed the marchers several blocks back to a church, hitting them with clubs. One policeman swung a rubber hose wrapped in barbed wire.

Finally the attacks stopped. Ambulances raced back and forth between churches and hospitals. Lewis was hospitalized with a fractured skull. Ninety other marchers were treated for gashes, broken bones, and other injuries.

The ruthlessness and the violence of that day shook the American people. Protests were held in different cities all over the country. President Lyndon Johnson, who had been hesitant to support the civil rights activists in their struggle for equality, finally saw the need to act.

"The American public had already seen so much of this sort of thing, countless images of beatings and dogs and cursing and hoses," Lewis wrote. "But something about that day in Selma touched a nerve deeper than anything that had come before."[4]

Johnson stunningly announced that he would ask the U.S. Congress for a law guaranteeing the right to vote for everyone, regardless of skin color. Johnson told the nation that the attacks on peaceful protestors in Selma were a crucial turning point in American history.

"At times history and fate meet at a single time in a single place to shape a turning point in man's unending search for freedom," he said in a national television speech. "So it was at Lexington and Concord. So it was a century ago at Appomattox. So it was last week in Selma, Alabama. The issue of equal rights for American Negroes is such an issue. And should we defeat every enemy,

President Bill Clinton, center, led a march across the Edmund Pettus Bridge on March 5, 2000, to mark the 35th anniversary of "Bloody Sunday."

In the 35 years since "Bloody Sunday," African Americans have made progress that was once unimaginable. Not only have blacks been able to vote, but they have also won elective office throughout the United States. John Lewis, who was beaten unconscious on "Bloody Sunday," was elected to the U.S. House of Representatives in 1986.

and should we double our wealth and conquer the stars and still be unequal to this issue. Then we will have failed as a people and as a nation."[5]

It was one chapter in the amazing story of the American civil rights movement, a period of American history which was filled with stories of bravery and heroics. Even Hollywood got into the act when *To Kill a Mockingbird*, a film about a lawyer who stands up to racial injustice in a small southern town, won three Academy Awards in 1962. In a short amount of time, many barriers to equality between white and black Americans were removed. But 50 years after the movement started, racial prejudice still festers. The problem dates back to the colonial era, when slaves from Africa were bought and sold like cattle.

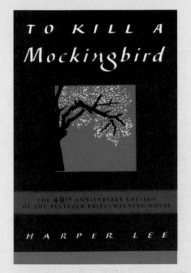

The issues of race and civil rights were hot topics in 1960 when first-time novelist Harper Lee's *To Kill a Mockingbird* was published. Lee set her story in the 1930s, but it nonetheless had a major impact on the 1960s.

The action takes place in a small Alabama town, similar to the one in which Lee grew up. The narrator is a young white girl named Scout. Scout's father, Atticus Finch, is a lawyer and a member of the state legislature.

Many of the white people in the town become upset when Atticus Finch defends Tom Robinson, a black man. Robinson is accused of raping a young white woman who lived near him. The drama in the book is heartrending. At one point, Finch spends the night sitting in a chair in front of the jail to make sure nobody tries to break Robinson out of jail and kill him. Such lynchings of black men were common throughout the South in earlier days. When a mob appears—apparently planning to lynch Robinson—Scout recognizes one of the members. She starts talking to him about his legal problems and his son. The man turns out to be the leader of the mob and they all leave.

Finch skillfully shows at the trial that Robinson is innocent, but the all-white jury finds him guilty. While his case is being appealed, Robinson tries to escape from a prison camp. He is shot and killed.

The book and the successful movie starring Gregory Peck as Atticus Finch were entertaining. But they were also important because they showed the injustice of racism. They made a hero out of a lawyer who believed everyone should be treated equally by the law.

To Kill a Mockingbird remains in print and is often considered one of the best American novels ever written. It not only tells a good story but also teaches an important lesson.

Gregory Peck and Harper Lee on the set of *To Kill a Mockingbird*

About 10 million Africans were brought to the Americas as slaves before the slave trade was outlawed in 1842. President Abraham Lincoln worked to abolish slavery in the United States in 1865.

After the Civil War, African Americans were no longer slaves. But the legacy of slavery lived on. African Americans were not, for the most part, allowed to become true citizens. They were kept out of public places such as hotels and restaurants. They were not allowed to attend "white" schools and colleges.

Why Civil Rights?

In 1758, Boyrereau Brinch was a 16-year-old boy living in the African countryside. He had just finished swimming in a pond one day with his friends. Suddenly slave traders swooped down on them. The traders bound and gagged him and 11 of his friends. Then they marched them to a port city. Soon they were taken aboard a ship. The boys were thrown into the bottom of the vessel, where they lay with scores of other captives amid human feces and rotten fish. "I was pressed almost to death by the weight of bodies that lay upon me; night approached and for the first time in my life, I was accompanied with gloom and horror,"[1] Brinch wrote many years later.

The slave trade had begun in the 1600s. It continued until it was outlawed internationally in 1842. Brinch was one of about ten million Africans who were captured and shipped to the Americas in horrible and often fatal conditions. "I was much bruised in many parts of my body, being most of the time gagged, and having no food only such as those brutes thought was necessary for my existence,"[2] Brinch wrote.

The voyage became known as the Middle Passage. Conditions inside the ships that made these voyages—which typically lasted from 25 to 60 days—were so awful that an estimated 16 percent of the captured Africans died in route.

Once the Africans were sold into slavery, their lives usually continued to be miserable. Cruel overseers sometimes whipped them mercilessly. Children were sold away from their parents. Some church groups and political leaders thought slavery should be outlawed after the American Revolution. The signers of the Declaration of Independence had written that "all men are created equal." But slaves were very important to the economy of the South, where they worked on large plantations harvesting cotton and other crops. Slaves also worked as servants, nurses, and in other positions. Sometimes they fought back against the slave owners. They also organized rebellions. The most common form of resistance was escape. About a thousand slaves fled to the north and to Canada every year.

The controversy over slavery grew in the early 1800s. Slavery was outlawed in some of the northern states. But the vast majority of the slaves lived in the South, where slavery was seen as not only legal and right but also approved by God and the Bible—or so the slave owners maintained. The conflict continued to grow until Abraham Lincoln, who was against slavery, was elected president in 1860. The southern states seceded, or withdrew, from the United States and formed the Confederate States of America.

The Civil War broke out the following year and continued for four years. More than 600,000 soldiers on both sides were killed. In the end, the South surrendered and the slaves were freed. African Americans rejoiced and looked forward to freedom and full equality with whites. For a short time after the war—a period known as Reconstruction—blacks were allowed to vote. Many were appointed or elected as officials in several states. But that system did not last. Gradually, white political leaders won back their power. They designed a system that separated blacks from whites in almost all areas of southern life such as schools, restaurants, and work places. Even public water fountains were designated "white" and "colored." They also took away almost completely the right of African Americans to vote. The system became known as "Jim Crow," which was taken from the name of a black slave character in a popular traveling minstrel show.

Black people did not sit quietly while their hard-won rights were taken away. They objected, and filed lawsuits. Many were based on the 14th Amendment to the U.S. Constitution. The amendment says that everyone is under the law, regardless of race. These efforts received a blow in 1896. In the case known as *Plessy v. Ferguson*, the U.S. Supreme Court said that segregation was legal as long as equal facilities were provided for blacks. The ruling was a big defeat for lawyers who were trying to persuade the courts that African Americans should be treated with justice.

At the turn of the century, the situation for blacks in the United States was grim. Between 1900 and 1915, more than 1,000 blacks were lynched, or killed by mobs. Thousands more were beaten and tortured. An African man, Ota Benga, was displayed in the Bronx Zoo's primate area along with a gorilla and an orangutan. But change was coming, however slowly. W.E.B. Dubois received his doctorate from Harvard University in 1895 and went on to become an important black intellectual. He and a group of people who were mostly white formed the National Association for the Advancement of Colored People (NAACP) in 1910.

In the 1930s, Adolf Hitler was leading Germany toward war —a war in which he hoped to establish the domination of white Germans over Europe. He wanted to use the 1936 Olympic Games, which were held in Berlin, as a way of demonstrating the superiority of the German people. But the dominant figure at those Olympics was a black athlete from Alabama named Jesse Owens, who won four gold medals in track and field. More than a million African Americans fought against Hitler and his racist allies in World War II even though the U.S. armed forces were segregated. When they returned home to the United States, they often expected more equal treatment for themselves and their children.

Little by little, African Americans began winning some rights. In 1946 President Harry S. Truman ordered the end of military units

"The problem of the 20th century is the problem of the color line," W.E.B. Dubois wrote in the *The Souls of Black Folk* in 1903.

Early African American intellectuals like W.E.B. Dubois laid the groundwork for the Civil Rights Movement. Dubois, however, became disillusioned with the lack of progress for blacks in the United States. He renounced his American citizenship and died in exile in the African country of Ghana in 1963.

divided by race. This was a big step for a society that remained mostly divided along racial lines. Jackie Robinson became the first black professional baseball player to play in the major leagues when he joined the Brooklyn Dodgers in 1947. In 1954, after a long legal campaign led by the NAACP, the U.S. Supreme Court ruled in a very important case called *Brown v. Board of Education* that segregated schools are illegal. The Supreme Court ordered communities across the country to allow African-American children to study in the same schools as white children.

Brown v. Board of Education was a big step toward equality, but there was a massive reaction against it. Many public schools were closed. Private, white-only schools were formed. Mobs and violent demonstrations attempted to deter black children from

attending all-white schools. The reaction against *Brown v. Board of Education* showed there was still a long way to go before anything like true black-white equality could come into existence. Two cases show how strong the prejudice against black people remained.

Carl and Anne Braden, a white couple, helped a young black couple buy a home in a white neighborhood of Louisville, Kentucky, in 1954. Enraged white people bombed the house. Carl and Anne Braden were arrested on charges of sedition—trying to overthrow the government of the state of Kentucky! Carl Braden was sentenced to 15 years in prison and was only released after the U.S. Supreme Court ruled in his favor eight months later. No charges were ever filed in the bombing of the house.

Owens and other outstanding black athletes have done a great deal to advance the cause of Civil Rights throughout recent American history.

Jesse Owens went to the Olympics in Nazi Germany in 1936 and won four gold medals.

The following year, Emmett Till, a 14-year-old Chicago boy visited relatives in Mississippi. He was brutally tortured and murdered because he might have said "Bye, baby" to a white woman shopkeeper. The killers were arrested and taken to trial. The all-white jury took only an hour to find them not guilty. One of them, J. W. Milam, was asked afterward why they had killed the teenager. He replied, "Well, what else could I do? He thought he was as good as any white man."[3]

African Americans had been suffering such treatment for a long time. The stage was set for a change.

Jackie Robinson was the first African American to play Major League Baseball in the United States.

When Robinson first took the field as a member of the Brooklyn Dodgers, fans jeered and complained. But Robinson won them over with stellar performances both on the field and at bat.

Linda Brown was a seven-year-old girl growing up in Topeka, Kansas. Because she was black, she had to walk six blocks to her bus stop, and then ride the bus for an hour and 20 minutes to her all-black school. Her white neighbors went to a nearby, all white school.

Situations like Linda's were common throughout the United States. African American children often attended schools without heat or indoor plumbing. Their teachers were paid less than the teachers at the white schools. Linda's father, Oliver Brown, sued the school board in Topeka, Kansas. The U.S. Supreme Court combined the Brown case with other lawsuits involving unequal education.

Thurgood Marshall had grown up in Baltimore and attended Lincoln University in Chester County, Pennsylvania. He applied to the University of Maryland law school and was turned away because he was African American. He studied law at Howard University and soon after graduating went to work as a lawyer for the National Association for the Advancement of Colored People. Marshall stated the case for making unequal education against the law in 1952. Two years later, Chief Justice Earl Warren released the court's unanimous opinion outlawing segregated schools. His famous words were: "Does segregation of children in public schools solely on the basis of race . . . deprive the children of equal educational opportunity? We believe that it does."

Warren ordered federal judges throughout the United States to supervise the desegregation of public schools. The ruling brought a harsh reaction from white opponents to segregation. They formed organizations to prevent the integration of the schools. They started whites-only private schools and pledged to fight desegregation lawfully. There were cases of violence against supporters of integration.

The process was very slow. Linda Brown continued to attend her black elementary school. Although in 1955 she attended an integrated junior high. Even today, experts say American public education remains segregated, but the Supreme Court ruling in *Brown v. Board of Education*, which made it illegal to purposefully separate white and black children, was a huge step forward.

Integrated classrooms took years to achieve

E. D. Nixon only had a sixth-grade education, but he had been active in his all-black union, the Brotherhood of Sleeping Car Porters, for many years. He believed strongly that if people organized, worked together, and protested non-violently, they could change unfair laws. When he heard that Parks had been arrested, he saw the case as an opportunity. As soon as he had helped Parks get out of jail by signing for her bail, he asked her if he could organize a protest against the arrest. "We can break this situation on the bus with your case,"[2] Nixon told Parks.

Parks knew she was putting herself in danger and would probably lose her job, but she agreed with Nixon. Years later, Parks said people often believed that she did not get out of her seat because she was old and tired. But they were wrong. "I was not tired physically, or more tired than I usually was at the end of the working day. I was not old, although some people have an image of me as being old then. I was forty-two. No, the only tired I was, was tired of giving in."[3]

Nixon called Jo Ann Robinson, an English professor at the all-black Alabama State College and the president of the Women's Political Council, an organization of black women. For years, Robinson had wanted to do something about the way black people were treated on the bus. Six years earlier she had absentmindedly sat in the front of a bus on her way to the airport. The driver got up from his seat, came over to her and held up his hand as if he was going to hit her. He shouted, "Get up from there! Get up from there."[4] Robinson was horribly humiliated.

Robinson and Nixon decided to call for a boycott—a protest involving mass refusal to use a service or buy something—of the buses on the next Monday, December 5. Robinson typed out a short statement explaining the need for the boycott. It said, "Negroes have rights, too, for if Negroes did not ride the buses, they could not operate. Three-fourths of the riders are Negroes, yet we are arrested, or have to stand over empty seats. If we do not do something to stop these arrests, they will continue. The next time it may be you, or your daughter, or mother."[5]

Robinson stayed up all night making tens of thousands of copies of the handbill. She arranged for students to pass out the flyers at schools throughout Montgomery. Ministers met Friday night and agreed to preach on Sunday morning in support of the boycott. But leaders were still afraid the black people of Montgomery would not respond. They knew people had to get to work and to school. They knew that many were afraid to protest. Monday morning dawned dark and cloudy. It looked as though boycotters were not only going to have to find a new way to get where they were going, but also that they were going to get wet.

But like Rosa Parks, the black residents of Montgomery were ready to protest. They walked to work, found rides, or rode in taxis. The buses were almost empty. A young man who had just moved to Montgomery to be the pastor of the Dexter Avenue Baptist Church was sitting in his kitchen drinking coffee when a bus that was normally full of black passengers went by his house. Martin Luther King, Jr. could not believe his eyes. The bus was empty.

King and the other ministers met to plan the future of the boycott. King was new in town and had not been politically active. He was only 26 years old and busy with his young family and his new church. But the other leaders saw King's inexperience as an asset. They thought he could bring a fresh perspective and fresh ideas to the city's black leadership. They talked a somewhat reluctant King into serving as president of the new Montgomery Improvement Association. They argued about whether the boycott should continue, and decided to let the people vote at a mass meeting that night.

King was not well known when he spoke that night, but his carefully chosen words resounded. "We are impatient for justice, but we will protest with love," King said. "If you will protest courageously and yet with dignity and Christian love, when the history books are written in future generations, the historians will have to pause and say 'There lived a great people—a black people—who injected new meaning and dignity into the veins of civilization.' This is our challenge and this is our overwhelming responsibility."[6]

Over the next weeks and months, the boycott took an amazing turn. The African Americans of Montgomery continued to stay off the buses. They walked or found rides all through the winter and the next spring and summer. They were still walking when fall came around again. The white leadership of Montgomery took desperate measures to break the boycott. They jailed the leaders. They harassed drivers who provided boycotters with rides. King's house was firebombed.

Finally, more than a year after the boycott started, the United States Supreme Court ordered the buses desegregated. It had been a long, hard struggle. And it had been non-violent. It would eventually be seen as a spark that would ignite a non-violent revolution throughout the South. As historian Harvard Sitkoff wrote, "Out of it would come a towering leader, a new kind of Southern black leadership, an effective strategy for social change, and a determined spirit that Jim Crow could be ended, that life could be better."[7]

It took time for the spirit of the boycott to spread throughout the South. Though there were other boycotts and protests, the system of segregation continued to rule the South. It would not go away easily.

In 1957, a federal judge ordered the school board to allow black students in Little Rock, Arkansas, to attend Central High School under a plan to desegregate the school district. White parents formed mobs outside the school and threatened to kill the nine black students who had been accepted into the school. "This is a criminally frivolous dispute, absolutely unworthy of this nation," commented writer, James Baldwin. "Educated people, of any color, are so extremely rare that it is unquestionably one of the first tasks of a nation to open all of its schools to all of its citizens."[8] The governor of Arkansas, bowing to pressure from the segregationists, ordered the National Guard to the school to help keep the students out.

Finally, President Dwight Eisenhower ordered the 101st Airborne Division to the school to make sure the nine students would be allowed to study. But the crisis dragged on for two years as the governor closed the schools and tried to lease them to a private school corporation to keep the races separate. Finally, the schools were reopened and integrated in 1959.

By then, Martin Luther King, Jr. had formed a civil rights organization called the Southern Christian Leadership Conference. But not even King's leadership could spark a national movement. Frustrated students, who are unknown, took the civil rights movement and broadened it until it reached all over the country.

Joseph McNeill, a seventeen-year-old freshman at North Carolina Agricultural and Technical College, wanted to eat at the bus terminal in Greensboro, North Carolina, on January 31, 1960. "We don't serve Negroes here,"[9] the waitress told him. That night, McNeill talked about how tired he was of such treatment with three of his fellow students. They talked about how slowly the progress toward equality was moving. Finally, McNeill said to his friends, "We've talked about it long enough, let's do something. But what can we do?" The room grew quiet as the four young men thought. Then McNeill said, "We should go in and ask to be served and sit there until they do."[10]

They decided to target lunch counters at downtown stores. Segregation at these lunch counters was particularly galling. Black people were allowed to shop at the stores, but they could not sit down, order a sandwich or a cup of coffee, and relax like white customers could. The next day the four young men bought some school supplies at the F.W. Woolworth store in downtown Greensboro. Then they sat down at the store's lunch counter and asked for coffee and dough-

Angry whites assaulted the African American students who "sat-in" at lunch counters throughout the South to protest segregation.

The sit-in movement spread like wildfire throughout the South. African American university students, sometimes after months of training in non-violence, and sometimes on the spur of the moment, went to "whites-only" lunch counters and politely asked to be served. They were arrested in droves.

nuts. The waitress refused and went to find the manager. The manager tried to convince them to leave. A small crowd of other customers gathered when they realized a protest was going on.

One woman supported the students. "Ah, you should have done it ten years ago. It's a good thing you're doing," she said.[11] She was alone in her approval. Other white people called them nasty names. An African-American woman who worked as a dishwasher at the lunch counter was horrified. She said, "This counter is reserved for white people, it always has been, and you are well aware of that. So why don't you go out and stop making trouble?"[12]

The students remained seated until the store closed. News of the "sit-in" spread quickly through campus. That night 50 students met and decided to continue the protest. There were so many of them that they also occupied seats at another store down the street. City leaders agreed to negotiate with the students, but only offered to partially desegregate the lunch counters. The students began occupying the store lunch counters again. The store owners had 45 of them arrested.

In Nashville, Tennessee, students had been studying non-violence and planning to protest against the city's segregated lunch counters. When they heard about the sit-ins in Greensboro, the Nashville students launched a massive, non-violent campaign of sit-ins at the city's lunch counters. John Lewis, who had grown up as the son of poor farmers in rural Alabama, was one of the leaders of the sit-in movement there. It was the first time he challenged segregation. "I was nervous," he wrote in his memoir. "We were all nervous. We didn't know what to expect. All my life I'd heard, seen and obeyed the rules. You can't use that library. You can't drink at that fountain. You can't go in that bathroom. You can't eat in that restaurant. I hated those rules but I'd always obeyed them."[13]

At first the students were ignored. When they continued to occupy the lunch counters, the store owners began to get desperate. White onlookers started getting mean. White teenagers attacked the protesters. Police came. They did not arrest the attackers, but instead took the protestors to jail and charged them with disorderly conduct. More students came to sit quietly at the lunch counters. They were also arrested. Soon the jail was full of students. They refused to pay bail and remained in jail, singing and chanting, "Jail without bail." Adults backed up the students by refusing to shop in the downtown stores.

The sit-in movement snowballed across the South. Students in more than 100 cities followed in the footsteps of the protesters in Greensboro and Nashville. It took time, but the store owners usually gave in and agreed to serve blacks and whites together at the same lunch counters.

The students had won an important victory. But there was a long way to go. They could not sit in regular seats at movie theaters. They were banned from many restaurants. Most important, African Americans were still prevented from voting in community after community across the South. They faced some difficult questions about the future of their movement, which was large but not coordinated. The sit-in movement was an example. It had been carefully planned in some cities but was more spontaneous in others.

Ella Baker, a long-time civil rights activist, saw a need to bring students together and help them organize their efforts. She scheduled a meeting on Easter weekend in 1960 and hoped that a hundred leaders might show up. Instead more than 300 came, including white students who wanted to support the civil rights cause. The students named their new group the Student Non-Violent Coordinating Committee, also known as SNCC. They had to decide what to do next.

Ella Baker devoted her life to the Civil Rights Movement.

Baker was one the unsung heroes of the Civil Rights Movement. She worked for the NAACP in the 1940s and for Dr. Martin Luther King, Jr. at the Southern Christian Leadership Conference in the 1950s. When the sit-in movement began, she brought the students together and helped them begin their own organization, the Student Non-Violent Coordinating Committee.

FYInfo

FOR YOUR INFORMATION

As the civil rights movement drew attention to the reality of racism in the United States in the 1950s and 1960s, Americans across the country turned to the books and articles of James Baldwin, a young black writer from New York City. His writings beautifully explained the struggle of black people under racism, and called on white people to assume the responsibility for change.

James Baldwin

"This man traveled the earth like its history and its biographer," wrote poet Amiri Baraka. "He reported, criticized, made beautiful, analyzed, cajoled, lyricized, attacked, sang, made us think, made us better, made us consciously human."[6]

When Black Muslim leaders Elijah Muhammad and Malcolm X drew thousands of followers by preaching that blacks were superior to whites, Baldwin published a long article on the phenomenon. The article was expanded into a book, *The Fire Next Time*, which told of Baldwin's harsh criticism of racism and his belief that separatism was not the solution. "The glorification of one race and the consequent debasement of another—or others—always has been and always will be a recipe for murder," Baldwin wrote.[7]

Baldwin was born in 1924 in the Harlem section of New York City to a single mother, Emma Burdis Jones. His mother married David Baldwin, the pastor of a small church, when he was three. At first Baldwin loved the church, and he began preaching sermons when he was only 14.

But at the age of 17 he lost his faith in religion. He decided he did not like the way some pastors lived comfortably while members of their churches struggled in poverty. He finished high school and began working in factories and restaurants while he tried to establish himself as a writer. The outlook for a young black writer in New York City in the 1940s was grim. He was harassed by police and white people.

He moved to Paris in 1948, where his career flourished. He returned to the United States to write about the civil rights movement, but mostly lived in Paris until he died in 1987, mourned as one of this country's most eloquent chroniclers of the "color line."

James Farmer founded the Congress of Racial Equality in Chicago in 1942.

Farmer was a key organizer of the "Freedom Rides" across the South in the early 1960s. When African Americans tried to make equal use of interstate buses and bus stations—as ordered by the U.S. Supreme Court in 1960, they were threatened, beaten, and jailed.

Violence and Voting

The U.S. Supreme Court helped the activists plan their next move. On December 5, 1960, the United States Supreme Court ruled in *Boynton v. Virginia* that blacks and whites could not be separated in transportation between states. James Farmer, who had been one of the founders of the Congress of Racial Equality in Chicago in 1942, knew that the Supreme Court ruling was not being followed. Blacks were beaten and jailed when they tried to sit in the front of buses belonging to companies such as Greyhound or Trailways. And contrary to the law, they could not eat at the bus terminals.

Farmer wanted to push the bus companies to follow the law by organizing a "Freedom Ride." This was a mixed group of black and white activists who would ride through the South together, trying to sit in the front of the buses and eat at the bus terminals. Farmer wrote letters explaining his plans to the head of the FBI and U.S. Attorney General Robert Kennedy. He recruited activists such as John Lewis, one of the student leaders in Nashville, and Jim Peck, an older white man who had been active in the civil rights and anti-war movements for 30 years.

The first Freedom Ride began in May 1961. It proceeded peacefully from Washington, D.C., through Virginia and North Carolina and into South Carolina. At the bus station in Rock Hill, South Carolina, Lewis approached the men's bathroom with the "white" sign on it. A few young white men warned him away, but Lewis said, "I have a right to go in there on the grounds of the Supreme Court decision in the *Boynton* case."[1] One of the men swore at him. Then they began beating Lewis and the other Freedom Riders. Police officers finally stopped the attacks. Rather than making arrests, they simply told the attackers to leave. One officer said, "All right boys, y'all've done about enough now. Get on home."[2] The Freedom Ride continued but the reaction only got more violent.

In Anniston, Alabama, a huge mob attacked the bus and slashed its tires. Someone in the crowd threw a firebomb at the bus and it began to burn. At first the riders were trapped inside. Then an undercover police officer waved a pistol at the crowd and the riders were allowed off the bus. A few were beaten before they could escape. Freedom Riders on other buses were also beaten. The beatings and the burning of the bus created a huge uproar, but the situation became even worse. Students throughout the United States were inspired by the courage of the Freedom Riders. At Albany State College in southern Georgia, students were arrested after they tried to buy tickets at the bus station. One of the students, Bernice Johnson Reagon, discovered for herself and many others the roll that music plays in encouraging protestors and reaffirming their commitment to nonviolence.

As Attorney General, Robert Kennedy was responsible for making sure the Supreme Court's rulings were followed. He sent an official of the Department of Justice, John Seigenthaler, to try to organize protection for the Freedom Riders. Alabama Governor John Patterson told Seigenthaler the Freedom Riders would not be harmed. But when Seigenthaler met a bus carrying Freedom Riders at the bus station in Montgomery, Alabama, a mob attacked him, news reporters, and the Freedom Riders. Someone hit Lewis with a wooden crate and he fell to the ground unconscious. When Lewis regained consciousness, he found the attorney general of Alabama standing over him, charging him and the other Freedom Riders with the crime of disturbing the peace.

Kennedy called Dr. Martin Luther King, Jr. to ask the Freedom Riders to stop. It seemed impossible to control the violence. He asked for a cooling-off period. But Farmer refused. "I asked Dr. King to tell Bobby Kennedy that we'd been cooling for 350 years, and that if we cooled off any more, we'd be in a deep freeze,"[3] he said.

The Freedom Riders decided to continue on to Mississippi, even though, as one Rider said, "everyone on that bus was prepared to die."[4] While they were not attacked in Jackson, Mississippi, they were arrested and taken off to a famously cruel prison called Parchman. It was a relief not to be beaten. It was outrageous to be sent to prison for simply riding a bus. More and more people joined the Freedom Rides. They were also sent to prison. Finally, on September 22, the government issued rules requiring blacks to be treated equally with whites in all bus stations and interstate buses.

Little by little, the old system of discrimination was being dismantled. But activists still had not confronted the biggest issue: the right to vote.

Technically, any citizen of the United States had the right to register, or sign up, as a voter in his or her home town. That right was supposed to be guaranteed by the U.S. Constitution. But across the South very few blacks had actually been allowed to register. White officials prevented blacks from registering by giving them impossible tests to take, by charging them high fees (known as poll taxes), or by simply threatening or beating them.

Medgar Evers grew up in Decatur, Mississippi, and fought in World War II. After the war, he and his brother were allowed to register. But on Election Day in 1946, they were met by a mob of white people carrying guns and knives. "We fought during the war for America, Mississippi included. Now, after the Germans and the Japanese hadn't killed us, it looked as though the white Mississippians would," Evers said. "We knew we weren't going to get by this mob."[5] He took a job as the Mississippi field secretary for the

NAACP. He investigated killings of African Americans in Mississippi, which were often dismissed by white police as "accidents."

Evers and others began persuading African Americans to attempt to register to vote. They also tried to get local white officials to allow them to register. Evers knew it wasn't going to be easy. "The white man won't change easily," he said. "Some of these people are going to fight hard. And more of our people could get killed."[6]

Evers was very brave. He continued his work after a small bomb was thrown at his house. When people called his house to threaten him, he would often talk to them politely and try to change their minds. On the night of June 12, 1963, he was shot to death as he walked into his house. Byron de la Beckwith, a member of a pro-segregation group called the White Citizens' Council, was arrested and charged with the murder after police found his fingerprints on the murder weapon. Two juries were deadlocked and refused to convict Beckwith, and he was released. He remained free until 1989, when he was tried again, found guilty, and sentenced to life in prison.

Evers' killing came amidst a wave of violence directed at activists, African Americans, and white people who supported civil rights. In Birmingham, Alabama, police attacked demonstrators with fire hoses and dogs. Martin Luther King, Jr. was thrown in jail, where he wrote a 19-page letter that has become famous for its eloquent call for a change in white America. "Perhaps it is easy for those who have never felt the sting of segregation to say, 'Wait,' " King wrote. "But when you have seen vicious mobs lynch your mothers and fathers at will and drown your sisters and brothers at whim; when you have seen hate-filled policeman curse, kick, and even kill your black brothers and sisters, there comes a time when the cup of endurance runs over, and men are no longer willing to be plunged into the abyss of despair."[7]

The continued protests and the continued violence against the demonstrators convinced President John F. Kennedy to propose a new law that would make segregation illegal. When Kennedy was first elected, he had not been a major supporter of civil rights. That had changed. He was horrified by the violence directed against the activists and was convinced that the government needed to do more.

Civil rights leaders organized a massive demonstration in Washington to push for the passage of the bill. The marchers would also call for the integration of schools and better job opportunities for African Americans. Organizers hoped to have 100,000 people show up for the march and rally.

The historic event, which was held on August 28, 1963, attracted about 250,000 people. About 60,000 of them were white. The day was beautiful and there were no problems with either marchers or police. John Lewis, who was by then the chairman of the Student Non-Violent Coordinating Committee, summarized the peaceful determination of the protesters: "By the force of our demands, our determination, and our numbers, we shall splinter the South into a thousand pieces and put them back together in the image of God and democracy."[8] Dr. King delivered his famous "I Have a Dream" speech, reminding everyone of the seriousness of the cause. People left the protest full of hope about the future, and confident that change would come.

But the bloodiest attack in the history of the civil rights movement was just a few days away.

Members of the Ku Klux Klan, a secret racist society that opposed equal treatment for blacks, planted a bomb in the Sixteenth Street Baptist Church in Birmingham on Youth Sunday, September 15. Denise McNair, 12, Addie Mae Collins, 14, Carole Robertson, 14, and Cynthia Wesley, 14, were killed and many others were injured. Two black male teenagers—Virgil Ware and James Robinson —died of gunshot wounds later that day. Robinson was shot by a white police officer. It was clear that King's "Dream" of a time when people would not be judged by the color of their skin was a long time away.

Martin Luther King, Jr. hugs a supporter after the Civil Rights Bill was passed by the U.S. Senate.

Civil Rights activists paid dearly but little by little they won better laws and a commitment from the federal government to enforce the laws. But progress was often slow.

While the Civil Rights Bill was under consideration by Congress, President Kennedy was assassinated in Dallas, Texas, on November 22, 1963. His vice president, Lyndon B. Johnson, became president.

Kennedy's death was a blow, but Johnson supported the struggle of African Americans. He pushed for passage of the Civil Rights Bill and signed it on July 2, 1964. He used the nation's outrage about the violence in Selma the following year to help pass the Voting Rights Act. It prohibited poll taxes and other means used to prevent blacks from voting. The civil rights movement had accomplished so much. It seemed that it could do even more.

But instead, those who had worked together began to argue with each other. The Vietnam War began to get more attention from activists. Non-violence began to lose its appeal.

FYInfo

FOR YOUR INFORMATION

Bernice Johnson Reagon was born in Albany, Georgia, on October 4, 1942. She grew up singing in her parents' African-American church. She loved music, but she did not understand its power until she became involved in the civil rights movement.

She was a student at Albany State College when some students were arrested for trying to buy bus tickets from a sales window reserved for white passengers. She helped plan a protest march. During the march, she began to sing an old African American spiritual song that went, "Over my head/I see trouble in the air." She changed it to "Over my head/I see freedom in the air." That night, when she and the other protesters had been arrested and sent to jail, they kept singing. The songs filled them with a sense of power and community.

Bernice Johnson Reagon

The next day, Reagon realized that her voice was deeper and stronger. She became a leader of the Freedom Singers, a group that sang at civil rights marches and meetings. She was suspended from school for her activities, but that suspension became an important part of her education. She became a full-time singer and activist.

Later she completed her studies at Spelman College. After graduating in 1970, she entered Howard University, where she earned her doctorate in U.S. history. She went to work at the Smithsonian Institute in Washington, D.C., studying African-American music and culture and developing concerts and exhibitions. She also taught at the American University and at Spelman College and wrote several books.

She founded Sweet Honey in the Rock, a famous women's singing group that uses only their voices and percussion instruments. They perform songs they have written themselves and classic songs of the civil rights and peace movements. In 1989, Reagon won a $500,000 grant from the John D. and Catherine T. MacArthur Foundation. She used the money to create an award-winning radio series called *Wade in the Water: African American Sacred Music Traditions*.

Reagon—as a performer and as a scholar—has probably done more than any other American to demonstrate and document the role of music in the civil rights struggle.

Malcolm X was born Malcolm Little in Omaha, Nebraska, in 1925. His father died when he was six, and he fell into a life of crime. He spent most of his 20s in prison.

When African Americans became impatient with the way non-violence was answered with violence in the 1960s, they began paying more attention to the leadership of people like Malcolm X. When Malcolm X first rose to national prominence he denounced white people as the enemy of African Americans. However, he began to change his ideas after a trip to Africa in 1964. Malcolm X was assassinated on February 21, 1965.

CHAPTER 5

The Rise of Extremes

Martin Luther King, Jr., who spoke so beautifully of the importance and the power of non-violence, became known as the most important civil rights leader as the 1960s progressed. In 1964, he was summoned to Norway to receive the Nobel Peace Prize.

As the attacks on civil rights workers continued, however, King and nonviolence began to lose their popularity and influence. Another important black leader named Malcolm X angrily denounced white America as he urged African Americans to become Muslims. Malcolm X was assassinated by followers of a rival Muslim leader on February 21, 1965. John Lewis, who believed strongly in non-violence, lost his position as chairman of the Student Non-Violent Coordinating Committee in May 1966. His replacement was Stokely Carmichael, who pushed more aggressive tactics and called for "Black Power."

Meanwhile, thousands of young American men were being drafted into the military to fight in Vietnam. King and other civil rights activists continued to try to organize non-violently for peace and civil rights, but anger at the lack of progress, the war in Vietnam, and the constant attacks on civil rights workers continued to build. Blacks rioted in the streets in 1967, especially after speeches by Carmichael and another SNCC leader, H. Rap Brown. Martin Luther King, Jr. said, "The bombs in Vietnam explode at home. They destroy the hopes and possibilities of a decent America."[1]

H. Rap Brown was one of the SNCC leaders who steered the organization away from non-violence.

Toward the end of the 1960s, the civil rights movement lost momentum. The Vietnam War raged and leaders like Martin Luther King, Jr. and Robert F. Kennedy were assassinated. The Civil Rights movements' victories still stand as remarkable achievements in American history.

The following February, more than a thousand black garbage workers went on strike in Memphis, Tennessee. They left their jobs because of the low pay and poor working conditions. Two workers, Echol Cole and Robert Walker, had been killed when a garbage truck malfunctioned and crushed them to death. King went to Memphis to help organize a march in support of the garbage workers' strike. But the march was a disaster. People broke windows and looted stores. For the first time in his life, King was escorted away from a march for his own safety. King felt terrible about the march's descent into violence. He vowed to return to Memphis to organize a peaceful march.

The march was set for April 4, 1968. The night before, King spoke to a large crowd. He was somber and, in hindsight, it seemed as though he knew he would not live for long. "We've got some difficult days ahead," he said. "But it doesn't matter with me now. Because I've been to the mountaintop. And I don't mind. Like anybody, I would like to live a long life. Longevity has its place. But I'm not concerned about that now. I just want to do God's will. And He's allowed me to go up to the mountain. And I've looked over. And I've seen the promised land. I may not get there with you. But I want you to know tonight, that we, as a people, will get to the promised land."[2]

The next day King stepped out onto the balcony of his room at the Lorraine Motel. He was shot by a sniper and killed. The nation grieved for King and his planned peaceful march was held in Memphis—as a memorial for him. But there were riots in other cities, and it seemed as though King's dream would die with him.

Richard Nixon, who was against the integration of schools and neighborhoods and promised "law and order" instead of "civil rights," easily won the 1968 presidential election against Hubert Humphrey, who had supported civil rights. The civil rights movement may, indeed, have died with King's murder but its ideals held. Progress—albeit slow and painful—has continued. John Lewis himself serves as an example. He was elected to the U.S. House of Representatives from Georgia's Fifth District in 1986 and has been continually re-elected. He is often considered the conscience of the House. On May 17, 2004, Lewis and many others celebrated the 50th anniversary of the historic *Brown v. Board of Education* decision, which ordered the end of separate schools for black and white children. The anniversary came at a time when the American people continue to struggle with the issue of racism. African Americans still face unemployment, poverty, and unequal education.

"This is why we cannot give in, we cannot give up, we cannot give out . . . until the promise of the Brown decision is fully realized," Lewis said on the floor of the U.S. House of Representatives. "We have come a long way, but we have a distance to go before we lay down the burden of race in America."[3]

Malcolm X is often remembered as the man who presented a contrast to Martin Luther King, Jr.'s emphasis on interracial brotherhood and nonviolence. When King gave his famous "I Have a Draeam Speech," Malcolm X said, "While King was having a dream, the rest of us Negroes were having a nightmare." It is true that Malcolm X's background and beliefs were very different from Martin Luther King, Jr.'s.

Malcolm X was born Malcolm Little in Omaha, Nebraska. His father was an outspoken supporter of rights for black people who was killed—probably to silence him—in 1931. Malcolm's family fell apart and he moved to Boston at the age of 14. He joined a gang and was sentenced to prison for burglary as a young man. While in prison, he became a Muslim. When Malcolm left prison, he dropped his last name, which he said was a legacy of slavery, and became Malcolm X. Malcolm X's thoughts were always interesting and he spoke well. He gradually became a prominent minister in the Nation of Islam and was assigned to lead the Muslims in Harlem, New York. He attracted many followers with his strong criticism of white America and his insistence that Black people improve themselves by helping each other.

As he became more and more popular, he made statements that increasingly angered Elijah Muhammad, the head of the Nation of Islam. When President John F. Kennedy was assassinated in 1963, Malcolm X said the killing was an example of the "the chickens coming home to roost." He believed that Kennedy and previous presidents had not done enough to prevent violence against blacks, and that failure had led to the violence boomeranging back to the president. Elijah Muhammad told him he must not make any more public statements without his permission.

Malcolm X left the Nation of Islam and made a pilgrimage to Mecca, in Saudi Arabia. There he had an important change of philosophy. He and other black Muslims had always preached black separatism, but in Mecca he saw the possibility and the importance of the unity of all races. He returned to the United States, with a plan to start a secular, or non-religious movement, that would unite African Americans with white and Hispanic allies. He organized a rally and had just begun speaking when he was assassinated by three men who were later linked to the Nation of Islam.

It was a sudden end to a life that had been remarkable, and seemed to be on the verge of becoming even more remarkable.

Chronology

1954 U.S. Supreme Court strikes down the separate-but-equal standard allowing schools to be divided by race in the famous decision known as *Brown v. Board of Education.*

1955 Rosa Parks is arrested for refusing to surrender her bus seat to a white passenger, which begins the historic Montgomery Bus Boycott.

1957 President Dwight D. Eisenhower orders the 101st Airborne Division to allow nine black students to enter Central High in Little Rock, Arkansas.

1960 Four students ask to be served at the Woolworth lunch counter in Greensboro, North Carolina, marking the beginning of the sit-in movement.

1963 Martin Luther King, Jr. writes the *Letter from a Birmingham Jail*; the 6,500-word document becomes a famous symbol of the civil rights movement; Martin Luther King, Jr. and other leaders speak before 250,000 people in the historic March on Washington; James Baldwin publishes *The Fire Next Time*, an important collection of essays on the issue of race.

1964 President Lyndon B. Johnson signs the Civil Rights Act, which prohibits discrimination in public accommodations, bans discrimination by employers and unions, and provides aid to communities that are desegregating their schools; Martin Luther King, Jr. is awarded the Nobel Peace Prize.

1965 Bloody Sunday, when 90 people are injured as Selma Sheriff Jim Clark's men attack a march; Malcolm X is assassinated; President Johnson signs the Voting Rights Act.

1966 James Meredith, who became the first black student at the University of Mississippi in 1962, is shot and wounded as he tries to march from Memphis, Tennessee, to Jackson, Mississippi.

1968 Martin Luther King, Jr. is assassinated on the balcony of a motel in Memphis, Tennessee.

1971 White civil rights lawyers Morris Dees and Joseph Levin, Jr. begin the Southern Poverty Law Center, a non-profit law office that works to implement civil rights law across the United States.

1972 The Raza Unida Political Party, which arose from the Mexican American civil rights movement in Texas, fields a slate of candidates led by Ramsey Muñiz as candidate for governor. The party wins a remarkable six percent of the vote.

1983 Harold Washington becomes the first African American mayor of Chicago. Other major American cities also elected their first black executives in the 1980s.

1993 Thurgood Marshall, a giant of American Civil Rights law, who was a lawyer for the NAACP and the first African America to serve on the U.S. Supreme Court, dies.

2000 President Bill Clinton leads marchers across the Edmund Pettus bridge in Selma, Alabama, on March 5, 2000, for the 35th anniversary of "Bloody Sunday," which led to the Voters Rights Act of 1965

2004 Notable African-American scholar Henry Louis Gates, Jr. calls for a new civil rights movement within the black community in his PBS film and book, *America Behind the Color Line: Dialogues with African Americans.*

2005 On January 17, Martin Luther King, Jr. day, Americans of all colors and ages performed community service in honor of the slain civil rights leader. Leaders have urged students and others to make the day "a day on, not a day off."

Timeline in History

1865 Slavery is abolished in the United States after the Civil War; African Americans are given rights during Reconstruction, but those gains are gradually taken away.

1896 The Supreme Court rules that segregation is legal under the justification of "separate but equal" in *Plessy v. Ferguson.*

1905 The Niagara Movement, the precursor to the National Association for the Advancement of Colored People, is formed.

1914 World War I begins.

1918 World War I ends.

1920 Women win the right to vote when the 19th Amendment to the U.S. Constitution is passed.

1929 The Great Depression begins with the crash of the stock market.

1933 Franklin D. Roosevelt is elected as U.S. president and begins to combat the Depression with many government programs.

1939 World War II begins when Germany invades Poland.

1941 The Japanese attack on Pearl Harbor prompts the United States to enter World War II.

1945 Harry S. Truman, who became president after Roosevelt died in office, orders the dropping of atomic bombs on Hiroshima and Nagasaki.

1950 The U.S. State Department revokes the passport of Paul Robeson, an African-American actor and singer who had denounced American racism and supported the communist Soviet Union.

1954 The McCarthy era begins to come to a close when the U.S. Senate censures Senator Joseph McCarthy, who had been leading an investigation of communist beliefs among Hollywood figures, singers, artists, government employees, and writers.

1963 President John F. Kennedy is assassinated in Dallas, Texas; Vice President Lyndon Johnson becomes president.

1968 Senator Robert F. Kennedy is assassinated while running for president; Shirley Chisholm of New York becomes the first black woman to be elected to Congress.

1971 About 500,000 people demonstrate in Washington, D.C., on April 24 against the Vietnam War.

1974 President Richard Nixon resigns after the Watergate scandal.

1979 Iranian students seize the U.S. Embassy in Tehran and hold the hostages for 444 days.

1986 Martin Luther King, Jr. is honored with a national holiday.

1991 President George Bush sends soldiers to the Persian Gulf to free Kuwait from Iraqi occupation.

1995 A bomb in Oklahoma City kills 168 people.

1999 President Bill Clinton is impeached on charges of lying about a sexual relationship outside of his marriage.

2001 Terrorists hijack four airplanes; two crash into the World Trade Center Towers in New York City, a third crashes into the Pentagon in Washington, D.C., and the fourth crashes in rural Pennsylvania.

2003 President George W. Bush sends American soldiers to Iraq in an effort to bring democracy to the Middle Eastern country.

2005 U.S. President George W. Bush begins a second four-year term. Iraq holds its first free election in more than 50 years.

Chapter Notes

Chapter 1 Bloody Sunday in Selma

1. John Lewis, *Walking with the Wind: A Memoir of the Movement* (New York: Simon & Schuster, 1998), p. 326.
2. Ibid., p. 328.
3. Ibid., p. 329.
4. Ibid., p. 331.
5. Ibid., p. 339.
6. Lisa Rosset, *James Baldwin* (Danbury, CT: Grolier Inc., 1991), p. 67.
7. James Baldwin, *The Fire Next Time* (New York: Dial Press, 1963), p. 96.

Chapter 2 Why Civil Rights?

1. Benjamin Prentiss, *The Blind African Slave* (St. Albans, VT: Harry Whitney, 1810), p. 72.
2. Ibid.
3. Sara Bullard, *Free at Last: A History of the Civil Rights Movement and Those Who Died in the Struggle* (New York: Oxford University Press, 1993), p. 45.

Chapter 3 The Birth of a Non-Violent Revolution

1. Juan Williams, *Eyes on the Prize: America's Civil Rights Years, 1954–1965* (New York: Viking, 1987), p. 66.
2. Harvard Sitkoff, *The Struggle for Black Equality: 1854–1980*. Toronto: Harper & Collins, 1981), p. 43.
3. Lynn Olson, *Freedom's Daughters: The Unsung Heroines of the Civil Rights Movement from 1830 to 1970* (New York: Scribner, 2001), p. 108.

4. Williams, p. 61.
5. Ibid., p. 68.
6. Ibid., p. 76.
7. Sitkoff, p. 44.
8. James Baldwin, *Nobody Knows My Name*. New York: The Dial Press, 1961, p. 101.
9. Ibid., p. 69.
10. Ibid., p. 70.
11. Ibid, p. 70.
12. Ibid., p. 71.
13. John Lewis, *Walking with the Wind: A Memoir of the Movement* (New York: Simon & Schuster, 1998), p. 94.

Chapter 4 Violence and Voting

1. John Lewis, *Walking with the Wind: A Memoir of the Movement* (New York: Simon & Schuster, 1998), p. 142.
2. Ibid.
3. Juan Williams, *Eyes on the Prize: America's Civil Rights Years, 1954–1965* (New York: Viking, 1987), p. 146.
4. Harvard Sitkoff, *The Struggle for Black Equality: 1854–1980* (Toronto: Harper & Collins, 1981), p. 109.
5. Williams, p. 208.
6. Ibid., p. 218.
7. Ibid., p. 189.
8. Lewis, p. 224.

Chapter 5 The Rise of Extremes

1. Harvard Sitkoff, *The Struggle for Black Equality: 1854–1980*. (Toronto: Harper & Collins, 1981), p. 219.
2. Ibid., p. 221.
3. Representative John Lewis, "Brown v. Board of Education," *Congressional Record* (May 17, 2004), H3057.

Glossary

bail (BALE)
Money paid in order to leave jail until a trial is held; also referred to as "bond."

debasement (dee-BAYS-ment)
The act of lowering something or somebody in status or esteem.

discrimination (dis-krih-mi-NAY-shun)
The act of treating a person differently because of that person's race, religion, or some other factor.

doctorate (DOCK-tuh-rut)
The highest academic degree; often abbreviated as Ph.D.

ethical (EH-thi-cal)
Following a set of moral principles or values.

glorification (glo-ri-fi-CAY-shun)
The act of making something seem better than it actually is.

integration (in-tuh-GRAY-shun)
The act of allowing people of different ethnic or racial groups to be together in a social, educational, or work situation.

minstrel (MIN-strel)
A traveling show of music and comedy, often with white performers coloring their faces black.

racism (RAY-cism)
The belief that one's race is superior to or better than others.

segregation (seh-gri-GAY-shun)
The separation of an ethnic or racial group from another group.

seminary (SEH-mih-nair-ee)
A school that trains people to work as religious leaders.

For Further Reading

For Young Adults

Andryszewski, Tricia. *The March on Washington, 1963: Gathering to be Heard.* New York: Alfred A. Knopf, 1996.

Bankston, John. *Coretta Scott King and the Story of the Coretta Scott King Award.* Hockessin, DE: Mitchell Lane Publishers, 2003.

Haskins, James. *Freedom Rides: Journey for Justice.* New York: Hyperion, 1995.

Lee, Harper. *To Kill a Mockingbird.* New York: Little Brown & Company, 1988.

Levine, Ellen. *Freedom's Children.* New York: Penguin, 1993.

Myers, Walter Dean. *Malcolm X: A Fire Burning Brightly.* New York: HarperCollins, 2000.

Polakow, Amy. *Daisy Bates: Civil Rights Crusader.* North Haven, CT: Linnet Books, 2003.

Powledge, Fred. *We Shall Overcome: Heroes of the Civil Rights Movement.* New York: Macmillan Publishing Company, 1993.

Siegel, Beatrice. *The Year They Walked: Rosa Parks and the Montgomery Bus Boycott.* New York: Simon & Schuster, 1992.

_____. *Murder on the Highway: The Viola Liuzzo Story.* New York: Macmillan Publishing Company, 1993.

Works Consulted

Reporting Civil Rights - Part One: American Journalism 1941–1963. New York: Literary Classics of the United States, 2003.

Reporting Civil Rights - Part Two: American Journalism 1963–1973. New York: Literary Classics of the United States, 2003.

Baldwin, James. *The Fire Next Time.* New York: Dial Press, 1963.

Bullard, Sara. *Free at Last: A History of the Civil Rights Movement and Those Who Died in the Struggle.* New York: Oxford University Press, 1993.

Lewis, John. *Walking with the Wind: A Memoir of the Movement.* New York: Simon & Schuster, 1998.

_____. "Brown v. Board of Education." *Congressional Record* (May 17, 2004), H3057.

McWhorter, Diane. *Carry Me Home: Birmingham, Alabama: The Climatic Battle of the Civil Rights Revolution.* New York: Simon & Schuster, 2001.

Oates, Stephen B. *Let the Trumpet Sound: The Life of Martin Luther King, Jr.* New York: Harper & Row, 1982.

Olson, Lynn. *Freedom's Daughters: The Unsung Heroines of the Civil Rights Movement from 1830 to 1970.* New York: Scribner, 2001.

Prentiss, Benjamin: *The Blind African Slave.* St. Albans, VT: Harry Whitney, 1810. (viewed on line at the University of North Carolina at Chapel Hill's website, Documenting the American South: http://docsouth.unc.edu/neh/texts.html#B)

Rosset, Lisa. *James Baldwin.* Danbury, CT: Grolier Inc., 1991.

Sitkoff, Harvard. *The Struggle for Black Equality: 1854–1980.* Toronto: Harper & Collins, 1981.

Williams, Juan. *Eyes on the Prize: America's Civil Rights Years, 1954–1965.* New York: Viking, 1987.

On the Internet

Civil Rights Law and History - U.S. Department of Justice
www.usdoj.gov/kidspage/crt/crtmenu.htm

The Martin Luther King, Jr. Center
www.thekingcenter.com/

The National Association for the Advancement of Colored People
www.naacp.org

The National Civil Rights Museum
www.civilrightsmuseum.org/

National Park Service's Martin Luther King, Jr. Historic District
www.nps.gov/malu/

The Tuskegee Syphilis Experiment
http://www.infoplease.com/spot/bhmtuskegee1.html

University of Southern Mississippi's civil rights oral history archives
www.lib.usm.edu/~spcol/crda/resources.htm

Index

101st Airborne Division   24
American Revolution   14
Baker, Ella   28
Baldwin, James   24, 29
Beckwith, Byron de la   34
Benga, Ota   15
Birmingham, Alabama   34
Boynton v. Virgina   31, 32
Braden, Carl and Anne   17
Brinch, Boyrereau   13
Brotherhood of Sleeping Car Porters   22
Brown, Linda   19
Brown v. Board of Education   16, 17, 19, 41
Brown, H. Rap   39, 40
Carmichael, Stokely   39
Centers for Disease Control   19
Civil Rights Movement
   early days of   21–25
   Freedom Rides   30, 31–33
   precursors of   16–18
   sit-ins   25–28
   voting rights   7–10, 31–36
Civil War   12, 14
Clinton, President Bill   10, 19
Cole, Echol   40
Collins, Addie Mae   35
Congress of Racial Equality   30, 31
Declaration of Independence   14
Dubois, W. E. B.   15, 16
Edmund Pettis Bridge   7, 10
Eisenhower, President Dwight   24
Evers, Medgar   33–34
F.W. Woolworth   25
Farmer, James   30, 31, 32
Greensboro, North Carolina   25, 27
Hitler, Adolf   15
Humphrey, Hubert   41
"Jim Crow"   14, 24
Johnson, President Lyndon   9, 36, 42
Kennedy, President John F.   34, 36, 42
Kennedy, Attorney General Robert   31, 32, 40
King Jr., Martin Luther
   assassinated   41
   house firebombed   24
   formed the Southern Christian Leadership
     Conference   25
   "Letter from a Birmingham Jail"   34
   mediating Freedom Rides   32
   opposing the Vietnam War   39
   organizing the bus boycott   23
   preaching prior to assassination   40–41
   winning Nobel Peace Prize   39
Ku Klux Klan   35
Lee, Harper   29
Lewis, John
   "Bloody Sunday"   6–10
   elected to the House of Representatives   41
   losing chairmanship of SNCC   39
   participating in the sit-ins   27
   riding in Freedom Rides   30, 31–32
   speaking at the March on Washington   35
Little Rock, Arkansas   24
Lincoln, President Abraham   12, 14
Louisville, Kentucky   17
Lynching   15
Malcolm X   11, 38, 39, 42
McNair, Denise   35
McNeill, Joseph   25
Memphis, Tennessee   40, 41
Middle Passage   13
Milam, J. W.   18
Minh, Ho Chi   42
Montgomery, Alabama   21, 23, 24, 32
Montgomery Bus Boycott   20–24
Montgomery Improvement Association   23
Muhammad, Elijah   11, 42
Nashville, Tennessee   27
National Association for the Advancement of Colored
   People (NAACP)   15, 16, 19, 28, 33
Nixon, E. D.   22
Nixon, President Richard   41, 42
Olympic Games   15, 17
Owens, Jesse   15, 17
Parchman   33
Parks, Rosa   20–22, 23
Patterson, Alabama Governor John   32
Peck, Gregory   29
Plessy v. Ferguson   15
Reagon, Bernice Johnson   37
Reconstruction   14
Robertson, Carole   35
Robinson, Jackie   16, 18
Robinson, James   35
Robinson, Jo Ann   22
Rock Hill, South Carolina   31
Seigenthaler, John   32
Selma, Alabama   6, 9, 10, 36
Sixteenth Street Baptist Church (bombing)   35
Slavery   13–14
Smithsonian Institute   37
Student Non-Violent Coordinating Committee   28, 35,
   39, 40
Sweet Honey in the Rock   37
Syphilis   19
Till, Emmett   18
To Kill a Mockingbird   10, 11
Truman, President Harry S.   15
U.S. Supreme Court   15, 16, 31
Vietnam War   39
Voting Rights Act   36
Walker, Robert   40
Ware, Virgil   35
Wesley, Cynthia   35
White Citizens Council   34
Williams, Hosea   7, 8
World War II   15, 33, 42